EXPOSITORY BIBLE STUDY COURSE

LESSON AND SERMON PREPARATION

By

Cooper P. Abrams, III

Disclaimer

The author of this work has quoted the writers of many articles and books. This does not mean that the author endorses or recommends the works of others. If the author quotes someone, it does not mean that he agrees with all of the author's tenets, statements, concepts, or words, whether in the work quoted or any other work of the author. There has been no attempt to alter the meaning of the quotes; and therefore, some of the quotes are long in order to give the entire sense of the passage.

Address All Inquiries to:

Cooper P. Abrams, III
cpabrams3@gmail.com
435 452-181
Web Site: http://bible-truth.org

The companion book titled *"Biblical Principles For Interpreting God's Word"* is available from Dr. Abrams

Published by:
THE OLD PATHS PUBLICATIONS, Inc.
142 Gold Flume Way
Cleveland, Georgia, U.S.A. 30528

Web: www.theoldpathspublications.com
E-mail: TOP@theoldpathspublications.com

1.0

ACKNOWLEDGMENTS

It is possible that some information within this study is not credited to its source. This was not intentional. This study began in 1980, as a Sunday School teacher training course at Calvary Baptist Church in King, North Carolina. Thus, the first material was in the form of study notes meant for teaching that class. The course proved to be well received and has been taught many times since. This provided the need for a more useful form of the notes for the students, and this began the formal compiling of this material in this study. This study has been revised many times over that past years. An attempt has been made to go back give credit to sources in the form of footnotes. However, some may have inadvertently been left out. If notified the oversight will be promptly corrected in future printings. Thank you for understanding.

Special thanks to:

My faithful wife, companion and friend,
Carolyn

TABLE OF CONTENTS

PREFACE

WHY USE THIS METHOD OF BIBLE STUDY?

This course is a companion to the book "Biblical Principles of Interpretation" written by the author. This course presents a practical application of these principles.

Many books have been written on the subject of how to study the Bible. This method's value is that it teaches the expository method of studying Scripture, which focuses on an exegetical investigation of the Bible and shows the individual how to study the Word of God for himself.

The expository method of Bible study seeks to present <u>truths</u>, <u>concepts</u> and <u>principles</u> that are taught by a Scripture passage. God has given us His method of interpretation of His word. God method does not impose a meaning on a passage, but seeks the meaning from the words and gramma of the passage. The basis of true expository Bible study is a thorough "exegesis" of the passage. In exegesis, one seeks to investigate the literal meaning of each word of Scripture. The definition of each word is considered with its relationship to the other words in its context. ("context," refers to the verses before and after a verse and involves the environment, situation, and background in which you find a word or verse)

In using this method of Bible study, you will be researching and gathering material about passages of Scripture. This method will help you to develop a systematic plan to follow in studying the Bible. It centers on completing a work sheet where the information is recorded. In completing the Work Sheet, you will be amassing much information about the passage you are studying. All this accumulated information will help you to determine the correct meaning of a portion of Scripture. Knowing the meaning of a passage will enable you to discover the spiritual truths God wants revealed and their practical application in life.

At the heart of this study is the Biblical truth of the "verbal plenary inspiration" of Scripture. The doctrine of "verbal plenary inspiration" teaches that every word of Scripture is inspired by God. God used human writers who He directed through the Holy Spirit to record His Word. Under the inspiration of the Holy Spirit, they wrote what God wanted said without error. What they wrote, in the original manuscripts was exactly what God wanted to say.

The Bible proclaims this truth in these passages:

> *"All scripture is given by inspiration of God, and is profitable for doctrine, for reproof, for correction, for instruction in*

righteousness: That the man of God may be perfect, thoroughly furnished unto all good works." (2 Timothy 3:16-17)

"For the prophecy came not in old time by the will of man: but holy men of God spake as they were moved by the Holy Ghost." (2 Peter 1:21)

PROCEDURES AND METHOD

The true child of God has a longing to know the Bible. He needs to learn how to study the Bible for himself. This is vital! Our philosophy of Biblical education today appears to be what could be called "spoon feeding." The believer depends on his pastor, Sunday School teacher, or writer of a book to feed him spiritually. However, preaching, teaching and reading books **about** the Bible should be only part of one's spiritual diet.

Each child of God, in addition to being taught by others, should be able to study the Bible and learn its principles for himself. Modern disciples of the Lord Jesus should be able to go to God's Word and spiritually feed themselves and be able to defend his convictions from Scripture.

We all should be students of the Bible, and hone our skills in the Word of God that we might be better instruments to reach others for Christ. God has commanded each of us to be Bible students and teachers. Our responsibility is to **KNOW** the Word ourselves, that we might be able to feed our own spiritual souls by feasting the on the sincere meat of God's Word.

The love of God is the best motivation for the believer to follow Christ. This love comes from knowing God. We can only know Him from His Word, which is the Bible. This is the power of the expository method of Bible study. This method teaches the pure Word of God as the Holy Spirit guides, inspires and nourishes us as we study.

The emphasis of expository Bible study is in verse by verse examination of the Word of God. By using this method, after your study is complete, the correct interpretation and application of the verses will become clearer. You will be less likely to impose YOUR meaning on the Scripture or a meaning that is not correct. You will be letting God interpret His Word, and you will understand what God truly said and meant.

As you read this material - pray, ask God for strength, and for wisdom. Then make a personal commitment to put the amount of time and dedication into this study that will allow God to shape you into a more useful servant.

Remember, this method is not easy or quick. It is not a short-cut to Bible training. It will require time. Before you begin, realize that this could be the turning point in your becoming a better, more skillful Bible student. It could have an eternal benefit in the souls and lives of the ones God sends your way!

All Christians are teachers. We teach at home, work and in daily routines of life. Some Christians have the privilege to teach from pulpits; some in classes such as Sunday School and in Bible Study Classes. No matter where you are teaching this method will be of help to you. (See 2 Timothy 4:2)

For those without formal college training this course can teach them how to study the Bible. It will help the pastor whose training has been limited to topical sermon preparation learn the expository method. The Sunday School teacher after learning this method of study will be better able to teach from the Bible and be less dependent on prepared lessons. It will teach the believer to feed himself from God's Word and become confident in their knowledge of the Bible.

This book is divided into two sections. Chapter One will instruct you in use of the Expository Work Sheet that will guide you step by step toward learning the expository method of Bible study. Chapter Two, will deal with the literal method of interpreting Scripture. It will teach the principles which are the basis of the expository method of Bible study.

The Objectives of the Expository Bible Study Method

This is a practical, hands on course designed to develop Bible Study skills by learning how to research expositorily a verse or passage of Scripture.

The objectives of the method are:

1. To teach how to study and correctly interpret the Scriptures.

2. To teach how to develop a Sunday School lesson, devotional, sermon, or for personal study.

3. To become familiar with Bible study helps such as dictionaries, handbooks, and concordances.

4. To build confidence in one's ability to understand the Bible and to teach others.

The procedures of the method are:

1. The chief activity will be personal study and practice using the Work Sheet and course instructions to guide you.

2. You will be studying passages of Scripture in detail to decide what they are saying.

3. Practical hands-on use of Bible and Bible study helps will help build confidence.

4. You will learn how to start a good Bible reference library.

Recommended Bible Study Helps:

1. A Study or Reference Bible

2. A Bible Dictionary

3. A Bible Concordance

4. A Bible Handbook

5. Word Study Books.

(A detailed list of these books is found on pages 23-32)

May God richly bless you as you study.

CHAPTER ONE

EXPLANATION OF THE WORK SHEET

Introduction

The Work Sheet is your guide to properly studying a passage of Scripture. If you follow the outline of the Work Sheet, your study will naturally develop. Do not omit any section. This course will refer to the product of your study as a lesson or sermon. This course's primary goal is to teach the expository method of Bible study. It is an added benefit that it also teaches how to prepare a Bible lesson or sermon. Sometimes lessons are one sided, being either all application or all technical information and background. This course will teach how to use both to develop a well-rounded lesson that will be interesting and easier to teach.

The main reason we teach and study is to make a practical application of Scriptures in our lives. Often in a lesson or sermon, the context, technical information, and background of a passage is ignored. The result is the true application is missed, because the passage is not fully understood. With a proper understanding and presentation of the context, technical information and background, often the passage usually teaches itself. It is interesting and more important, if presents God's truth in a way that can be applied to our lives.

Another added benefit of this method is that it gives the teacher and Bible student confidence. When you stand before the class to teach or in your personal study of Scripture, you KNOW what the passage says and means! You know what God wants you to know.

Each step in the "Explanation of the Work sheet" corresponds numerically to the Work Sheet. The Work Sheet is a guide to lead you in fully examining the passage of Scripture you are studying. It may seem at first awkward, but as you continue to use it, you will begin to see its value. Remember this is not a short cut or quick method of Bible study - it requires time. Christ said, "Seek and you will find." This method of Bible study is for the "**seeker**" - who, by the way - will reap the blessings of being a "**finder**."

> *"Thy word have I hid in mine heart, that I might not sin against thee . . . I will meditate in thy precepts, and have respect unto thy ways. . . I will delight myself in thy statues . . .I will not forget thy word." (Psalms 119:11, 15-16).*

OUR PRAYER SHOULD BE:

"Open thou mine eyes, that I may behold wondrous things out of thy Law" (Psalms. 119:18)

CHAPTER TWO

A GUIDE TO BIBLE STUDY HELPS

This course will use Bible Study helps in investigating various passages of Scripture. The following is a list of recommended reference helps and a brief description of each one. We are very fortunate to live in this age when we have so many valuable aids to Bible study. These books will be a good addition to your library.

Only a few of the study helps available are listed below. If you were to have these books as a beginning library, you would have an excellent start on building a useful library.

Do not be discouraged if you do not have all the reference books listed. If all you have now is a Reference Bible, you have a great resource available to you. It would be a good investment to purchase at least one book in each category listed below. In time, you might like to have several Bible handbooks, dictionaries or commentaries. Building a library is a lifetime endeavor.

Where to Buy Study Helps and Reference Materials

There are many sources for Christians books, including local Christian bookstores. At Christian bookstores you will normally pay full retail price for the book. Compare the prices of several sources before you buy and look for sales. Buying used books, such as offered on Amazon.com will save you money. We need to be good stewards of the money God gives us to use. The following two companies consistently offer reference materials at reduced prices:

Amazon.com, Amazon Books,

http://www.amazon.com/books-used-books-textbooks/b?node=283155

Scripture Truth Book Company, P.O. Box 339, Fincastle, VA 24090.

http://www.scripturetruth.com/shop/custom.aspx?recid=1 - 540 992-1273

Christian Book Distributors, Box 3687, Peabody, MA 01961-3687-

http://www.christianbook.com/ .- 508 977-5000

A List of Study Helps and Reference Books

Bible Handbooks

Halley's Bible Handbook, Henry H. Halley, Zondervan Publishing House

Unger's Bible Handbook, Merrill F. Unger, Moody Press

A Bible Handbook is arranged according to the Books and Chapters of the Bible. It contains a wealth of information about the Bible. It includes, as the title page of Halley's Bible Handbook states, "A General View of the Bible, Heart thoughts of the Bible, Remarkable Archaeological Discoveries, Notes on Each of The Bible Books, Miscellaneous Bible Information, Notes on Obscure Passages, Related Historical Data, An Epitome of Church History, Suggestion on Church-Going."[1] This information is invaluable in understanding the historical situation of the Scripture you are investigating.

There are many pictures, charts and diagrams found throughout the handbook that greatly aids in understanding the historical situation of portions of Scripture. For example, the reference to Genesis 10-11, gives a great deal of information concerning Egyptian history, including the Egyptian dynasties, past wars, and chronology of the period. This

---

[1] **Error! Main Document Only.** Halley's Bible Handbook, by Henry H. Halley, Zondervan Publishing House, 1965, Title Page

background information will help you to understand the period of time between the Flood and Abraham.

Bible Dictionaries

Unger's Bible Dictionary, Merrill F. Unger, Moody Press, Chicago.

Zondervan's Pictorial Dictionary of the Bible, Merrill C. Tenney, Zondervan Publishing House, Grand Rapids, Mich.

Nelson's Illustrated Bible Dictionary, Herbert Lockyer, Thomas Nelson Publishers, Nashville, Camden, New York.

Holman Illustrated Bible Dictionary, Chad Brand, Archie England and Charles W. Draper.

A Bible Dictionary is an alphabetical listing of all the major words found in the Bible with their meanings. A Bible Dictionary is more like an encyclopedia than just a simple word dictionary. For example: it will list all the proper names found in the Bible, with not only its pronunciation and meaning, but also will give information about the various persons in the Bible that had that name with related Scripture references. A Bible Dictionary will furnish information on such things as money, tools, customs, geography, cities, towns and countries. It will list each Book of the Bible with an outline and historical data, such as the author, date, addressee, subject and content.

A Concordance of the Bible

Strong's Exhaustive Concordance of the Bible, James Strong, MacDonald Publishing Company.

Young's Analytical Concordance of the Bible, Robert Young, Wm. B. Eerdmans Publishing Company.

Layman's English-Greek Concordance, James Gall, Baker Book House, Grand Rapids, Michigan, 1975

The Englishman's Greek Concordance of the New Testament, George V. Wigram, Baker Book House, Grand Rapids, Mich, 1979.

A Bible concordance is an alphabetical listing of every word found in the Bible and lists every verse in which it is used. If you know only one word of a verse, you can use a concordance to find the reference you are looking for. The first two concordances listed above are "exhaustive concordances." This means that every occurrence of the word in the Bible is listed. Condensed concordances have only limited use, as they do not list every occurrence of a word in Scripture. Strong's is probably the most popular concordance. In addition to being a concordance, it includes a Hebrew and Greek dictionary of Bible word.

Strong has assigned each Hebrew and Greek word in the Bible with a number. This numbering system is used by most other reference books, making Strong's Concordance a must for Bible students.

The Layman's English-Greek Concordance lists all the English words of the Bible. However, under each English word is listed the various Greek words from which it was translated with references. For example: If you were to look up the English word "accompany" you would find that no less than five Greek words are translated "accompany" in our English Bible. Each of the five Greek words has a slightly different meaning. By looking up the definition of the Greek word in a word study book such as Vines Complete Expository Dictionary of Old and New Testament words, you would have a better understanding of the passage of Scripture.

The Englishman's Greek Concordance of the New Testament, is a Greek concordance, (written in English), arranged using the Strong's Concordance word numbering system. Without being able to read Greek, a word can be located in English in Strong's

Concordance and then using Strong's numbers can be used to find the exact Greek word in The Englishman's Greek Concordance. The Greek words are arranged alphabetically and each verse the Greek word is used in the New Testament is shown. This is invaluable in determining the exact Greek word used and its proper meaning.

Word Study Books

Vine's Complete Expository Dictionary of Old and New Testament Words, W. E. Vine, Merrill F. Unger, William White, Jr., Thomas Nelson Publishers. Nashville, 1984

Theological Word Book of the Old Testament, Harris, Archer, Waltke, Moody Press, Chicago.

Word Study Greek-English New Testament: with complete concordance, Paul R. McReynolds, Tyndale.

Word Pictures in the New Testament, A. T. Robertson, Baker.

Word study books list the words used in the Bible with their Greek or Hebrew meaning. (Hebrew for the Old Testament and Greek for the New Testament) These study helps are invaluable in determining the original meaning of the words of the Bible. Our English words were translated from Hebrew or Greek and often one English word was used to translate several words in the original language. It is important to know which Hebrew or Greek word the English word represents in order to determine its correct definition.

Commentaries

The Wycliffe Bible Commentary, Charles F. Pfeiffer, Everette Harrison, Moody Press, Chicago.

Matthew Henry's Commentary on the Bible, Matthew Henry, MacDonald Publishing Company, McLean, VA.

Romans, Donald Grey Barnhouse, Wm. B. Eerdmans Publishing Company, Grand Rapids, Mich.

The Bible Knowledge Commentary, An Exposition of the Scriptures by Dallas Seminary Faculty, Old and New Testament, John F. Walvoord, Roy B. Zuck, Victor Books, 1988. (Caution: Based on the New International Version of the Bible)

A Commentary on the Holy Bible, Matthew Poole, Hendrickson.

A Commentary on the Old and New Testament, Jamieson, Fausset, and Brown, Hendrickson.

Thru the Bible. J. Vernon McGee, Nelson

A Commentary on the Book of Jude. Cooper P. Abrams, III, Bible Truth Book Store, http://bibletruthbookstore.com/.

A commentary is the written comments and explanatory notes of an author on Scripture. Many commentaries are available covering the entire Bible or just one Book. When consulting commentaries be sure to investigate the author. This information will be found on cover sheets of most books. Where the author went to school, the denomination he belongs to, what Bible version he uses, and other information will guide you in determining his position on the Scriptures. Just because a person writes, a commentary on Scripture is no assurance what he writes will be doctrinally sound.

Commentaries can greatly aid in studying the Bible, but be aware they can become a crutch if we are not careful. Use them to get different perspectives on a passage of Scripture. Be aware commentators can make errors in judgment and come to incorrect conclusions. The rule is to use them as a guide, but never as an authority. The Bible itself is our only authority. It is the Bible that judges whether the commentator is correct.

The three commentaries above are very popular and are representative of most commentaries. They would be a good addition to your library. The first two are commentaries on the whole Bible and are good "general" reference to the Scriptures. Verse by verse commentaries focus on a smaller portion of Scripture and will give more detailed information than would be possible in a commentary covering the entire Bible. Purchasing several commentaries on one book will help you get a better and wider perspective on the book you are studying.

Study Bibles

The Ryrie Study Bible, Charles Caldwell Ryrie, Moody Press, Chicago.

The Scofield Reference Bible, C. I. Scofield, Oxford University Press, New York.

The Thompson Chain Reference Bible, Frank Charles Thompson, B. B. Kirkbride Bible Co., Inc.

A Study Bible is one in which an author has written explanatory notes in the margins. Study Bibles will have much information that aids in understanding the Bible. Modern words are given for antiquated ones. Cross-references are included to guide the reader to other places in Scripture where the subject of the verse is found, or to parallel passages. Some contain abbreviated Bible dictionaries and concordances that can be very useful.

CHAPTER THREE

BEGINNING YOUR STUDY

To Begin:

Please read "Principles of Literal Bible Interpretation" by Cooper Abrams that is a companion book to this study. Read and become thoroughly familiar with the principles in this book. Understanding and applying these principles of Bible interpretation is vital in properly studying Scripture expositorily. It will greatly aid you by teaching eleven principles to guide you in correctly interpreting the Bible. Before you begin this study, take the time to digest the material in this book that is the foundation of Bible and expositorily presenting God's word.

AFTER YOU HAVE DIGESTED THE INFORMATION IN THE BOOK, BEGIN YOUR STUDY HERE.

YOU WILL FIND A MASTER COPY OF A WORK SHEET IN THE BACK OF THE BOOK. USE IT TO MAKE COPIES TO USE IN YOUR STUDIES.

WITH A COPY OF THE WORK SHEET IN HAND, FOLLOW THE INSTRUCTIONS BELOW:

THE SYMBOL ✐   DENOTES PLACES WHERE YOU WILL BE MAKING ENTRIES ON THE WORK SHEET AS YOU PROGRESS THROUGH THIS STUDY.

_____

_____

✐ Enter the today's date. In the future, it may be helpful to know when you made this study.

✐ SECOND: Enter the Scripture reference you will be studying. We will begin this lesson by studying Acts 9:1-31. This passage will be used as an example several times in this study.

✐ THIRD: Enter the title of the study if you have one at this time.

It may be better to assign the study a title after you have completed your work. The title should reflect the content of your studies and will be developed as your investigation proceeds. It should relate too and reflect what this lesson or sermon is about. A good title will spark interest in the message and cause your hearers to want to know what you will be teaching.

STEP I. <u>CONTEXT</u>

✐ Read the chapter (Acts 9:1-32) at least twice from the Bible. Be sure also to read the chapter(s) before and after the passage once. (Acts 8 & 10) Read the passage until you understand what it is generally about.

36

If you find that the wording of the passage is hard for you to understand it may be helpful to read the passage from another translation of the Bible such as, The New King James Bible (NKJV). The New King James Bible (NKJV) is the best modern translation; however, it falls short of being a trustworthy translation. Without question, the King James Version (KJV) is the best English translation of the Bible. All modern translations are based on the corrupt Greek text of Westcott-Hort "scholarship." The KJV has stood the test of time and has not been affected by so-called "modern scholarship" that omits passages of Scripture, mistranslates words, miss uses dynamic equivalency, and casts doubts on other areas of God's word.

The best practice is to look up each word in the text using a Greek-English Dictionary such as Vines Expository Dictionary of Old and New Testament Words. Leaning what each word means will reveal the meaning of the passage. There is more about this in this study.

PLEASE REVIEW THE SECTION ON "CONTEXT" IN CHAPTER TWO, BEFORE YOU CONTINUE YOUR STUDY.

(I) Who is the Book Addressed to or Who is about?

FIRST, determine to whom the book is addressed or who is it about. It is recognized that all Scripture is given for our benefit and is applicable in principle to all. However, here we are seeking to find to whom the passage was historically addressed when it was penned and/or what it was about.

a. Read the introductory material found in your reference Bible.

b. Consult Halley's or Unger's Bible Handbook or a Bible dictionary or better, read both to find historical or geographical information related to the passage.

c. In the Old Testament many of the books are written to Israel or about them, however, some are written to other nations.

For example: From the introductory material in Halley's Bible Handbook, you would find that the book of Obadiah is addressed to Edom and is a prophecy of its destruction. The information on the Psalms would indicate that they are generally all addressed to Israel and many are about David himself. You may find Books such as the Song of Solomon hard to pinpoint. It is a poem of Solomon's love for the Shulamite girl and the subject is not specifically stated. If you consulted Unger's Bible Dictionary it would include information on how Bible scholars have interpreted the book and give you a better understanding of who and what the book is about.

✎ Write the pertinent information you find in this blank. In Acts 1:1, the author addresses this

Epistle (letter) to "Theophilus." From your Reference Bible or Bible Dictionary you will find that this name means, "Dear to God" or "Friend of God."[2] Record what information you find about Theophilus. You will find also that the Book although is addressed to Theophilus it is written to the all Christians because it is a historical record of the foundation of the *ekklesia* or local church and how the church began.

Sometimes who the Book is written to is not clear. If you cannot be sure whom the Book is addressed to, then try to determine who or what it is about. The Gospel of John does not have an addressee. You should record this information and then find out whom or what is the book about. In consulting a Bible Dictionary, you would find the Book is a Gospel about the Lord Jesus and presents Him as the Son of God the Savior (John 20:30-31).[3] The Gospel of John is not a Synoptic Gospel as are Matthew, Mark, and Luke. Find out why. If you checked a Bible commentary, such as Matthew Henry, would will find the introductory information as well.

---

2. Ryrie Study Bible, Charles Ryrie, Moody Press, Chicago, page 1677.
3. Unger's Bible Dictionary, Merrill F. Unger, Moody Press, Chicago, Page 701.

✐ **Write this information down**. This could be important later in your study. Remember you are attempting to gather as much information about the passage as possible. Consider yourself on a treasure hunt making note of every clue you find. Sometimes what seems insufficient at first may later turn into a precious jewel of truth and help you understand more fully the spiritual message of the passage. The rule is record what you find. Later when you prepare your sermon or study you can decide to omit or exclude information you find.

(2) Who is the Chapter About or Addressed to?

NEXT, determine who the **Chapter** is addressed to or who is it about. The chapter could be addressed to or about someone other than who the book addresses.

✐ **In Acts 9:1-31, the chapter is about the Apostle Paul, who is called Saul here.**

Ask: Are these believers? If so, what kind, Jew or Gentile? Are they religious leaders as Scribes, or Pharisees? Was this person a political leader or held some public office? It will help you to determine the context of the passage to know whom it was written.

✐ **The book and the passage could be about the same person or subject. If that is the case, write that down.**

Examples: (Read each of the following passages of Scripture)

Gospel of John 4. Jesus is speaking to the Samaritan woman. (She was a half Jew)

Matthew 16. Jesus is rebuking the Pharisees and Sadducees

Luke 5:27. It is about the call of Levi, called Matthew.

Acts 1. Christ is speaking to the disciples

Acts 2. It is about the disciples gathered in the upper room.

Acts 10:23-48. Cornelius, a gentile, Roman Centurion

Acts 19:1-7. It is about Paul and his encounter with the disciples of John the Baptist.

The Book of Hebrews. It is addressed to Jewish believers who were in danger of turning from Christ and returning to Old Testament Judaism.

Hebrews 11. It is about the faith of Enoch, Noah, Abraham, etc.

If your study was in the Book of Galatians obviously, it was written to the "Galatians." You would record this in "STEP 1, CONTEXT, Item 1."

If it your passage was from Galatians Chapter 6, is about, a sinning brother. The Book is found to be generally addressed to the Church at Galatia, however Chapter six is addressing a more specific subject, that being a sinning brother.

(3) What is the Historical Situation of the Passage?

Consult your Bible helps to research the historical situation. Look in your reference Bible in the introductory material before the Book. Look for: (1) the date it was written; (2) the governmental situation; (3) local situation, and (4) what were the events surrounding the situation?

✎ **Acts 9:1-31, is the account of the conversion of the Apostle Paul. He was on his way from Jerusalem to Damascus to persecute the believers there. Christ appears to him in a blinding light and Paul becomes a Christian.**

Other Examples

If you were studying a passage in 1 Corinthians you would start by reading the passage and consulting several Bible study helps. You would find that the Book of 1 Corinthians was written in 56 AD. The Gospel was preached in Corinth on Paul's Second missionary journey in 50 AD. He lived with Aquila and Priscilla, preaching in the synagogue until those that opposed him forced him to move in a house next door. He was accused before the Roman Governor Gallio, but the charge was dismissed. There was gross sin in the church and much need of instructions. Paul was in Ephesus when he wrote to this young church.[4]

If 1 Corinthians 5:1-2, was your text, you would want to include that these verses deal with a problem of incest in the church there. Checking the chapter in Halley's Bible Handbook, you would discover that Paul mentioned this problem again in 2 Corinthians 2.

(4). What is the Major Subject?

✎ **In Acts 9:1-31, the major subject is the conversion of Paul.**

Read the passage carefully to find its subject. If it is not clear, read the verses before and after the verse. You could be in the middle of a discourse that began in earlier verses. If you have difficulty, deciding what is the Major Subject, consult your Reference Bible or Bible Handbook and look at the chapter headings.

Example:

2 Cor. 8:16-24. Various authors list the same subject, but word the chapter title differently:

Ryrie Study Bible: "Principles of giving"

---

4. The Ryrie Study Bible, page 1619.

The Scofield Reference Bible, "Part II. The collection for the poor" (3) The Messengers.

Halley' Bible Handbook: Chapters 8 and 9, Listed as, "Offering for the Mother-Church."

From these titles and from reading the text you will see that the major subject is "giving." Remember, this is YOUR study. If you see something different from what is in your Bible helps, write it down also. You may want to word the title differently.

(5) Who is the Author of the Book?

In section "3. The Historical Situation," you recorded information about the general historical situation of the passage. This section should list information about the author. A good source for this information would be the introductory material listed before the Book in your reference Bible. A Bible dictionary will give you much detailed information about the author. In some Books of the Bible, the author is not known. In some, there may be some question as to whom the name refers to due to there being several persons with the same name. A Bible dictionary will explore all the possibilities.

✎ **The Book of Acts was written by Luke, who was a physician and companion of Paul on his second missionary journey. Read the introductory information on the Book's** authorship. **Consult several Bible Helps in obtaining this information.**

Examples:

The Book of Romans? Paul - In Rome in prison

The Book of James? James the half-brother of the Lord and pastor of Jerusalem church. Hebrews? Unknown. Possibly was Paul.

Record any information about the author. Such things as who Bible characters were related to or their occupation adds depth to your study. A Bible Dictionary would furnish this information.

(6) Record any parallel references.

Check the margin of your reference Bible to see if it lists any parallel references to the verse or subject. Record them and <u>look up each reference</u>.

✎ **In Acts 9:1-31, you should find that your reference Bible refers to Acts 22:1-29, and Acts 26:9-19 as other accounts of Paul's conversion.**

In the Gospels, you would want to check a "Harmony of the Gospels." A "Harmony of the Gospels" is a chronological listing of the events in the Four Gospels. Each event in the Gospels is shown with the passages that refer to it in each of the Four Gospels.

Some reference Bibles have a "Harmony of the Gospels" in the back. They are found in book form such as, <u>A Harmony of the Gospels</u>, by A. T. Robertson.[5]

STEP 2. DEFINITION OF WORDS

Definitions of words that you do not know should be recorded here. Some words in the King James, are not understood today and have taken a different meaning. Check your Reference Bible's marginal notes and an English dictionary, such as <u>Webster's New World Dictionary</u>, for the meanings. If there is any doubt in your mind that you do not fully understand the meaning of the word, look it up!

✎ **In Acts 9:1-31, you might want to find out what the following words mean: V., "prick," V22, "confounded," V26, "assayed," V29, "disputed."**

Another way to determine the meaning is to look the word up in <u>Vines Expository Dictionary of the New Testament</u> (for the New Testament) or <u>Wilson's Old Testament Word Studies</u> (for the Old Testament). More in-depth studies of Old Testament Words can be found in the <u>Theological</u>

---

5. <u>A Harmony of the Gospels For Students of the Life of Christ</u>, A. T. Robertson, Harper & Row, Publishers,   New York, Evanston and London, 1950.

Wordbook of the Old Testament. If these are not available, you can look the word up in the dictionary of Strong's Bible Concordance.

To find the correct definition in Strong's follow these instructions: Find the word and then the verse where it is used. There will be a number to the right of the verse. Look up the number in the back of the concordance in the dictionary and it will give the meaning of the Greek or Hebrew word. Make sure that if the word is from an Old Testament reference use the Hebrew/Chaldee dictionary. A New Testament word should be located in the Greek Dictionary. If you have access to the Theological Wordbook of the Old Testament you will be able to find a much more detailed definition. It will be easier to find a word's usage by first finding the word in Strong's Concordance. Use the reference number found in Strong's and look it up in the Index of the Theological Wordbook, found in the back of Vol. II.**Example:** 1 Corinthians 5:6: Word "leaven."

Vines Expository Dictionary gives the meaning for "leaven" on pages 362-363.[2] It shows that in the reference, the Greek word is "ZUME" a noun. It means, "leaven, sour dough, in a state of fermentation, etc." Much information about the word is included. In referring to this passage it

---

6 Vines Expository Bible Dictionary of the Old and New Testaments, Nashville:Thomas Nelson, 1985, pp362-63.

states it literally refers to "implied corrupt practice and corrupt doctrine respectively." This information will greatly aid you in understanding the passage.

STEP 3. INFORMATION ON NAMES, CITIES, AND PLACES

Information on names, cities and places is important in understanding the Bible passage. Use your Bible helps such as your Bible dictionary and also maps to locate the places mentioned and record what you find.

Most reference Bibles have good maps in the back pages. One problem with these maps is there is no "Gazetteer" (an index of geographical locations). It would be good to purchase a good Bible atlas. This make finding geographical locations easy and fast.

✎ **In Acts 9:1-31. Find out what you can about Damascus. Locate it on a map. Verse 11, states that Paul was from "Tarsus." Where was this city? Find out who were the "Grecians" of verse 29. Do you know where "Caesarea" is located? If you do not know find out.**

Other Examples:

Names: Jacob: Means, "supplanter;" Joshua: Means, "salvation"

Place: Galilee: Northern area of Palestine, west of the Sea of Galilee.

City: "Hebron": On of the oldest cites of the world located west of the Dead Sea. Its name means, "league or confederacy." It is 19 Miles from Jerusalem. Situated at 3000 feet above sea level and 4500 feet, it is a choice place for growing grapes. Abram camped there, built an altar to God, and owned a parcel of land called "the field of Machpelah" where he buried Sarah. Later in the conquest of Canaan, the city was given to Caleb, to conquer. Hebron was David's capital city before he became ruler over all Israel.

STEP 4. ACTION AND RESULT!

As you read and study the passage, look for "Actions" and "Results." To understand this procedure first looks at the following examples:

✎ Acts 9:4-5. Subject: Paul's conversion.

"And he fell to the earth, and heard a voice saying unto him, Saul, Saul, why persecutes thou me? And he said, Who art thou, Lord? And the Lord said, I am Jesus whom thou persecutest: {it is} hard for thee to kick against the pricks. And he trembling and astonished said, Lord, what wilt thou have me to do? And the Lord {said} unto him, Arise, and go into the city, and it shall be told thee what thou must do." (Acts 9:4-6)

Note the what happened in these verses.

Example 1.

✎ **Acts 9:**

V4 **(Action)** Christ speaks to Paul

V5 **(Result)** Paul responds "Who are you Lord?"

(Action) Christ says "Jesus whom you persecute"

V6 **(Result)** "What will you have me do?"

Example 2:

Isa. 6: V1-4 Isaiah saw God's holiness!

V5 Isaiah sees his sinfulness and cries

"Woe is me"

V8 God asks, "Whom shall I send?"

Isaiah responds, "Here am I Lord, send me."

Note that the natural sequence of events was first an "Action" and then a response or a "result." Looking for the "action and result" in a passage of Scripture helps you determine what happened. You will see later how this will help you to find the spiritual truths God is giving us.

If you have trouble finding the Action and Result in a verse look for verbs in the verses.

Example 3.: II Thessalonians 3:1-5

V1 **(Action)** Paul said, "**Pray** for us."

(Note the verb is "pray")

(1. Gospel may have free course and not be hindered.)

(Result) You are to **pray** for what?

(2. V2. That Paul might be delivered from persecution of wicked men.)

V3 **(Action)** The Lord is **faithful**.

(Result) You are **protected** and **kept** from evil.

V4 **(Action)** The Lord **strengthens** you.

(Result) You are then able to successfully live for the Lord.

V5 **(Action)** The Lord will **direct** your hearts.

(Result) (1. Toward a greater love of God.

(2. Help you wait patiently for Christ.

Sometimes the Action or Result may not be confined to one verse. The Action could be in one verse and the Result continue over several verses.

What you are trying to do is to decide what each verse is telling you to do. The end result of this exercise is to find out what is the practical application of the verse or passage of Scripture.

Let's look at another example:

Acts 26:1-32

V1 **(Action)** Agrippa gives Paul permission to speak in his defense.

V2 - V23 **(Result)** Paul tells how he came to know Christ.

V24 **(Action)** Festus declares Paul is beside himself.

V25-27 **(Result)** Paul continues and addresses the fact that King Agrippa, a Jew was familiar with the Old Testament.

V28 **(Action)** Agrippa says, Paul you almost persuade me to be a Christian.

V29 **(Result)** Paul says he longed to see Agrippa and all there saved.

V30-31 **(Action)** Agrippa, Bernice and Fetus go aside and declare that Paul is not guilty of any crime.

V32 **(Result)** They kept Paul in bonds, because he had appealed to Caesar.

With practice you will be able to determine the Action and Result of a passage. Write down your findings and then go on to Step 5.

STEP 5. PRINCIPLES NOTED

After you find the ACTION and the RESULT of a passage you next seek to find the principles that are in the verses.

(Read the examples in Step 4: again)

A principle is a "fundamental truth, law, doctrine, or motivating force upon which others are based."[6a]

Principles are truths and remain the same in both the Old and New Testaments. Traditions of mankind change, as does customs, cultures, environments, governments and historical situations. A truth does not change. The application of a truth or principle may be different at one time in history than at another, but the principle does not change.

6a. Webster's New World Dictionary of the American Language, The World Publishing Company, Cleveland and New York, 1951, page 1158.

Here is an example:

The Old Testament clearly establishes the doctrine or principle of the separation of God's people from evil and idolatry. It is seen in God's command to the Children of Israel not to marry, enter into contacts or have close dealings with the sinful Canaanites. This principle, when it was obeyed, kept Israel from temptation and compromise. It kept them from being polluted by those who did not fear God. (Read Deut. 7:1-26)

In the instructions to the nation of Israel, God told them to destroy the altars, images and places of idol worship. (Deut. 7:5) This clear commandment of God is not practiced today. Should it be? Are we commanded by God to attack and destroy false and pagan churches of today?

Paul in 2 Corinthians 6:14-18, teaches the same principle. (Read this passage) The time, place, customs and situation are different, yet the principle is still true. What is changed is the application of the principle. Christians are not to be unequally yoked with unbelievers. Paul says, *"what fellowship or union can Christ have with the Devil?"* In verse 17, quoting Isaiah 52:11, Paul warns believers to come out from the world and be separate. Thus, the principle applied in the Church Age, means we are not to form close associations with unbelievers. Paul does not tell us, however to attack unbelievers.

54

This commandment in the Old Testament was to the Nation of Israel. It is based on the same principle as later revealed in 2 Cor. 6:14-18. In order to understand the relevance of the Old Testament Law to us today we must realize the Law was given to govern a nation. God's Law was Israel's "Constitution". Israel was a "theocracy". That means they were ruled by God. The Law that God gave Israel covered every area of life within their nation the same way nations today are ruled by their laws.

The commandments in the New Testament are written to a church. The church, which is made up of believers, is not a nation. We are ruled by the government of the nation in which we are citizens. We are not under the Old Testament Law which governed Israel. These Laws were for Israel. This does not mean the Old Testament Law has no application within the lives of Christians today! We are to obey the principles which formed the laws of God for the Nation of Israel.

To help in understanding this, let us look again at the principle of separation. Christians should live absolutely by the principle of separation from evil and evil doers, but we live in a different age. We are not a nation, but a group of believers, a church. It would be incorrect to try to apply to the church the application of the principles given in the Old Testament that dealt with separation. We are not to destroy idolaters and their places of worship! That commandment was given to Israel in the Old Testament, not to the New Testament church.

In order to find the principle in a passage look for a truth. From Deuteronomy 7:1-26 and 2 Corinthians 6:14-18 you would find the principle of "separation." In other words, "believers are to separate themselves from close relationships with the world." This is the truth presented by these verses.

There may be more than one principle found in the passage. Some could be more important than others. List all those you see. Later, if you see others and add them to your work sheet.

Example: Note that in 2 Corinthians 9:6-8, several principles are found.

"But this I say, He which soweth sparingly shall reap also sparingly; and he which soweth bountifully shall reap also bountifully. Every man according as he purposeth in his heart, so let him give; not grudgingly, or of necessity: for God loveth a cheerful giver. And God is able to make all grace abound toward you; that ye, always having all sufficiency in all things, may abound to every good work:" (2 Corinthians 9:6-8)

The overall principle is clear, "we should be freely giving to the work of the Lord. Other principles found there are (1) that if we, "give sparingly we shall reap sparingly." In verse 7, is the principle that (2) determines how much we are to give, mainly, "as a man purposes in his heart." The principle of (3) being a cheerful giver is also clearly presented.

Look for God's truths in this passage and record them on the work sheet.

✎ **Acts 9:1-8. There are several principles found in these verses.**

(1) Christ seeks the sinner. V3-5 Jesus appeared to Paul.

(2) You cannot run from God. V. "it is hard for thee to kick against the pricks". Paul tried to stifle his conscience. He knew he was doing wrong.

(3) Christ wants the sinner to serve Him. V6 The Lord told him to go into the city and he would be told what to do.

(4) When the sinner meets Christ, he should obey Him.

V8, Paul did as he was told.

Can you find more? Record the principles you find.

STEP 6. PROPOSITION (or APPLICATION)

After you determine what God did or said, you now determine what action you should take! This is then put into the form of a sentence that will become your "proposition." The proposition is also at times called the "application". We will use the word "proposition" in this study. You are "proposing" an action by your study.

Look at the principle you located in Acts 9. You should now determine what is the major objective of the passage of Scripture. This becomes the objective of your study. Ask the question? "What is this passage telling me to do?" How should this truth be applied to your life and the lives of those to whom you may teach this Scripture? This is why God gave us His Word.

God's Word should become a part of us and change our lives. Applying these Scriptures to our lives will mature us and make us more Christ like. Ask, "Why is God saying this to me?" "What is God wanting me to do?"

✎ **In Acts 9:1-8, Paul asked what Christ wanted him to do. Clearly, Christ wanted Paul to serve Him. Thus, "service" is the main application, or you could say the thought of this passage. You then form the application into a sentence that proposes something.**

Examples:

"Christ wants us to serve Him"

"We must serve Christ!"

"Christ calls us is to service."

Note that the above examples are all saying the same thing, but differently. The statements are proposing an action for you to take. The subject of this action is "service to the Lord." Another way of stating this action could be: "We must bow to the Lordship of Christ." Paul had, before he met Christ, openly and zealously opposed the work of Christ. But when he met Christ, he acknowledged Christ as LORD and vowed to serve Him.

Make your statement short, one sentence, and to the point! Have only one major application to a lesson or sermon. Concentrate the entire message on developing that one point. In the next two steps you will learn how to express the practical application of your proposition.

STEP 7 & 8. HOW AND WHY

[As you study these next two Steps record your findings on your Work Sheet. You will find that often there is not enough space on one sheet to write all you find. Use another piece of paper or another Work Sheet if you need more space.]

Please note that "Steps 7 and 8" are two different ways to present the same truth. If your proposition is: "Christ's call is to service," you should next ask the question: How can I serve Him? or Why should I serve Him?

Generally, "HOW" is better than "WHY," because it is tells us what we are to do. Sometimes "WHY" is best and fits the passage better. Try HOW first then WHY.

✐ **Acts 9:1-31. Proposition: or "We must serve Christ." Other ways to make this statement could be: "Christ's call is to service" or "When Christ calls us to service, we should obey." You see then, you can state the proposition in several ways.**

The proposition is taking the passage of Scripture and putting it in practical terms. It is telling us to DO something. The proposition is a simple statement of what the verse is telling us to do. Truth can be taught in great detail and depth, and yet not help the student of the Bible change his life. We must understand what action the Scripture is compelling us to take. The proposition of a passage is making the truth simple and practical so we can apply it in our lives. You could say that it is taking truth understood by the head, and turning it into directing the feet.

STEP 7. HOW?

Ask the passage of Scripture **"HOW"** can one apply the principle? What can one DO, to apply the truth in his life?

! Acts 9:1-20. Your proposition is, "We must serve Christ." You next ask the passage (9:5) "How can I serve Christ?" From the passage you see what Paul did and said and what the Lord's response was.

Make the answer in the form of a question, **HOW?** It asks the question: **"How can we serve Him?"**

From the passage we can find several ways to serve the Lord. The key to this procedure is using the word, "BY." If you ask how to do something, you naturally respond with a "by". How can I do this? "BY" doing this. . . Note how "by is used in the following example:

     1. (V.) **By** seeking to find out who Christ is (Who are you Lord?)

     2.(V6) **By** finding out what Christ would have us do, by asking, (What will you have me do?)

     3. (V8) **By** being obedient. (Paul went unto the city as Christ told him)

4.(V20) **By** testifying publicly (witnessing). (Paul straightaway preached in the synagogues)

This procedure becomes simple with a little practice.!

✎ **Now read the example again and note the answers to your questions in verses 5, 6-8, and 20. Sometimes your answers will be taken from several verses as shown here. Record your findings on the Word Sheet.**

STEP 8: WHY?

In asking **WHY**, we are seeking a reason or benefit to obeying the proposition.

Repeat the same procedure as you followed in Step 7, but now ask WHY instead HOW. Rephrase your proposition and ask "**Why** should I serve the Lord?" Your answer could be stated "**Because**: Jesus is the Christ, the Son of God and is our Lord." As you study each verse or passage of Scripture you for answers to your question "WHY."

An example of WHY? It asks the question: "Why should we serve the Lord?"

✎ **Acts 9:1-32. The proposition is "We must serve Christ!"**

Ask, "Why, must I serve Christ? Your answer can begin with, "Because. . ."

1. (V.) Because Jesus is the Christ, the son of God.

2. (V6-8, 20f) Because Christ has work for us to do.

3. (V32) Because service brings edification of the churches and men walk in fear of God.

STEP 9. YOUR OUTLINE

This is the final step in your preparation. Now you place all your information into a usable form.

ON THE WORK SHEET YOU MAY NOT HAVE SUFFICIENT SPACE TO PLACE YOUR

OUTLINE. IT MAY BE BEST TO PLACE IT ON ANOTHER SHEET OF PAPER.

Your outline should contain the following:

Title: Make your title interesting and let it say what your lesson is about.

✎ "God's Call - Man's Response"

Scripture: Read the passage. (Note any words which may need explaining)

✎ Acts 9:1-20

Proposition: State your proposition or application.

✎ "In Acts 9, we find from the account of the apostle Paul's conversion, the principle taught that once a man is saved, he is called into a life of service to Christ. This means you and I must serve Christ!"

✎ I. **Introduction:** In the introduction you prepare your hearers for the main lesson. You give them information they will need to know to better understand the context or local situation at that time in history when the Scripture was written.

Also, very effective are current illustrations or situations today that are relevant to your hearers which this passage addresses.

II. **State your first "How" or "Why" and then support it.** Support it first from the passage itself and then from other Scriptures. Reinforce your principle by using illustrations.

✎ II. **"We must serve Christ because He is our Savior.**

A. Jesus Christ is God. (John 1:1)

1. He died on the Cross for our sins. (I John 2:2)

2. Paul saw the Resurrected Lord Jesus. (Phil. 3:10)

B. Christ seeks the lost sinner and offers us mercy and forgiveness of our sins. (Rom. 5:8)

1. Even while Paul persecuted the believers Christ still loved him, and sought after Paul.

2. He seeks us today. (Rev. 3:20)

Quoting other Scripture references to support your principle or teaching greatly helps in presenting the truths found in our passage. Note these Scripture passages in the outline support the statement being made.

Illustrations are important to any good message or lesson! It helps clarify the truths you are presenting and also gives variety to your presentation. It makes it more palatable to your hearers.

There are many places to get illustrations. In fact, you can get them almost anywhere. Current world conditions, and news are good sources. Personal experiences you or someone you know has had are excellent choices. Many illustrations can be found in books of illustrations which you can purchase. One is the Encyclopedia of 7700 Illustrations, by Paul Lee Tan[7]. This book has

---

7. Encyclopedia of 7700 Illustrations, Paul Lee Tan, Assurance Publishers, Rockville, Md., 1979.

many illustrations which are cataloged and indexed by subject.

One note of caution. Books of illustrations are available to everyone and it is possible find the same illustration used by many preachers or teachers. This is also possible if you get your illustration from another's message or lesson. Illustrations which become well known and often used are not very effective when used.

Be honest if you use an illustration which you "made up" or borrowed. It is dishonest to infer that a made-up illustration is a true event or one you borrowed happened to you.

III. **State your next "How" or "Why" and support it same as II.**

✒ **"We must serve Christ because He has a purpose for our lives.**

IV. **Next Point.**

Continue on until you have 3 or 4 major points.

V. Conclusion: Restate the major points of your outline and lead the people to make the proper response.

CHAPTER FOUR

FOLLOWING IS AN EXAMPLE OF WHAT YOUR OUTLINE MIGHT LOOK LIKE:

The information found in the outline comes from your work sheet. There will often be more information on the work sheet than you can use. Chose the information that best supports your application.

Title: "God's call - Man's response"

Scripture: Acts 9:1-20

Proposition: "We must serve Christ"

I. Introduction:

A. Paul's background.

   1. Education - Studied under Gamaliel. (Acts 22:3, 26:4-5)

   2. Position - Pharisee of Pharisees, devoted Jew. (Gal. 1:4, Phil. 3:5)

   3. Name "Saul" (Acts 13:9)

   4. He was a Roman Citizen (Acts 22:28)

5. Birth place - Tarsus, busy Roman-Greek trade city in the north east corner of the Mediterranean Sea. Popular for manufacture of goat hair used in tent making. Paul was a tentmaker. (Acts 18:3)

B. Paul's religious activities.

1. Acts 7:58 - At Stephens stoning.

2. 8:3 As persecutor of the Church.

3. V26: l0-1 Paul describes how he persecuted the church, by beatings, imprisonment, murder.

4. Acts 9:1-3 Paul was on his way to persecute the Christians at Damascus.

II. To serve God we must accept Jesus Christ. Acts 9:4-5

A. It was Christ who sought Paul, Christ now seeks us.

1. Through preaching, teaching, and study of the Bible.

2. Christ came to seek and to save the lost.

B. Paul knew the authority of the One calling Him.

1. Paul's response was "Lord."

2. He fell on his face.

3. Holy Spirit's work is to illuminate the Word of God and convict us.

4. Paul knew the O. T. Scriptures concerning the coming Messiah.

5. Paul was very religious as evidenced by the way he persecuted those he thought were heretics.

C. Paul now accepted Jesus Christ is the Messiah the Son of God.

1. Everything now changed.

2. Paul began a new life of service.

III. We must willingly seek God's Will for our lives. Acts 9:6

A. Paul's response was "Lord what wilt thou have me to do?"

B. The call to salvation is a call to service.

1. Isaiah had a similar experience. Isa. 6:1-13

2. When the Lord asked, "Whom shall I send, and who will go for us?," he responded "Here am I, send me."

C. The Lord had a plan for Paul's life. Acts 9:15-16

1. The Lord has a plan for every believer.

2. It is seen the Great Commission. Matt. 28:19-20

3. It is seen in the gifts every Christian receives. 1 Cor. 12:4-11, 18, 27-28.

IV. We must be obedient to God's plan for our lives. Acts 9:6-8

A. Jesus told Paul to go into the city and there he would receive instructions.

B. Paul arose and immediately did as Christ said.

C. God's plan for Paul was reveal through another believer Ananias.

1. God told Ananias what was His plan for Paul.

2. To receive the instruction Paul first had to obey.

3. Obeying Christ's instruction he met Ananias and Paul received his sight again.

D. Paul then obeyed the first commandment to a new believer and was baptized.

V. We must share the Gospel with others. Acts 9:20-22

A. Paul was saved and immediately became a testimony for the Lord.

B. He boldly proclaimed that Jesus was the Messiah. Verse 22

<u>Continue on with your outline until all your points are exhausted.</u> Generally, three major points (How's or Whys) are enough. Include more if your study needs them.

After you make your first outline you should go back and read it again. You may see changes you can make which will make the outline clearer. You may make several revisions of an outline before it is ready to present.

CONCLUDING REMARKS:

Once you have completed your work sheet and outline, you should have a thorough knowledge of the passage. The truths you learned will help you in growing spiritually in the Lord. Further, you can now confidently address this passage with understanding and be able to explain it to others. You can also witness to someone, or stand before a class or congregation and correctly teach God's Word with confidence.

It will be well to realize that you probably have more information and material to teach or preach than can be taught in your allotted time. You will learn in time from experience how to consolidate your message or lesson and present it within your time period.

After you become familiar with this study method you will probably drop the use of the Work Sheet. It is only intended to be a crutch and a learning aid. As you learn the method it will become automatic for you to search the Scriptures and research the information the Work Sheet asks for. You will probably adapt it to your personal needs and study habits.

You will also soon be aware that as you use this study method your knowledge of the Word of God will grow. You will be becoming a useful tool that the Lord will use in bringing others to Christ and helping fellow believers to grow also.

✐ Now that you have gone through the Study Guide for the first time choose another passage of Scripture. Begin a new work sheet. Research the passage of Scripture as you have learned. Select passages of Scripture you are familiar with. Later as you grow more proficient, work on more difficult passages.

> *"Open thou mine eyes, that I may behold wondrous things out of thy Law"* (Psalms 119:18)

ABOUT THE AUTHOR

Dr. Cooper Abrams is a veteran missionary, pastor, church planter, and author working in the state of Utah since 1986. He and his wife Carolyn are missionaries sent by Calvary Baptist Church, King, NC and have been involved in seeing three sound Independent Baptist churches established in Utah since 1986 and assisting other churches in Utah, Wyoming, and Idaho.

He graduated from Piedmont Baptist College in 1981 with a Th.B. (Bachelor of Theology), and in 2000 with an MBS (Master of Biblical Studies). In 2013, he earned a PhD in Religion - Bible Major from Bethany Divinity College and Seminary.

He is an avid writer and has authored numerous articles, books, Bible courses, and six Bible commentaries. His has written many articles on apologetics, hermeneutics, Baptist History, The Pentecostal Movement, and Mormonism.

Most of his work is posted on his popular Internet web site, Bible Truth http://bible-truth.org. The website which was begun in 1996 currently averages thousands each month. The site is rated as one of the top two to five Baptist websites, out of thousands on the Internet.

He can be contacted at:
435 452-1716
http://bible-truth.org
cpabrams3@gmail.com

Calvary Baptist Church
P.O. Box 536
King, NC 27021